The Best Pet for Al

Bruno M. Frank
Illustrated by David Sheldon

A Harcourt Achieve Imprint

www.Rigby.com
1-800-531-5015

Al liked to talk to his Uncle Lou. He liked to know what went on at the zoo.

One morning Uncle Lou came by
in his truck.
He said, "You wanted a pet.
You are in luck!"

But an alligator is not the best pet!

Everything at Al's house was soon
very wet.

"I can't keep this pet," Al told Uncle Lou.
"I'm sending it back to you at the zoo."

The next morning Uncle Lou came back.
He had a new pet for Al and a big,
white sack.

But a polar bear is not the best pet!

Polar bears like things that freeze.
The cold made Al start to sneeze.

"I can't have a bear," Al told Uncle Lou.
"I'm sending it back to you at the zoo."

The next day Uncle Lou came by yet again.
He had a new pet in a big, long pen.

Al's room was no place for a moose!

What would Al do with a moose
on the loose?

"This moose is not the best pet,"
Al told Uncle Lou.
"Please stop sending pets from the zoo!"

14

So Uncle Lou sent something little and white.

"Thanks, Uncle Lou," Al said.
"A cat is just right!"